AROUND ST AUSTELL BAY

JOY WILSON

BOSSINEY BOOKS

Published in 1986 by Bossiney Books,
St. Teath, Bodmin, Cornwall.
Printed and bound by A. Wheaton & Co Ltd,
Exeter, Devon.

ISBN 0 948158 16 6

ACKNOWLEDGMENTS

The author and publisher would like to thank the following people for their generosity in lending the old photographs and picture postcards that have made this book possible:
Dorothy Beard, Jennifer Best, Gareth Bullen, Mrs Claydon and Mevagissey Museum, Brenda de Courcy, Mrs Graham Gullick, Mr and Mrs Ivor Herring, Phyllis Kendall, Terry Knight and the Ellis Collection, Kathleen May, Bob Over, Geoff Prettyman, Roger Penhallurick and the Royal Institution of Cornwall, Mr and Mrs P. Rashleigh, Dr A. L. Rowse, Iris Stephens, Leonora Trewin, Damaris Tremayne, John Truscott, H. R. A. Vivian, Beryl Whetter, Jane Williams, Ivy and Rose Young, EEC International, St Austell Brewery, Graham Rideout and Andrew Garner of Cameracraft, Truro, for his professional help.
The cover photograph of Mevagissey is by courtesy of the Royal Institution of Cornwall with colour tinting by Paul Honeywill.

About the Author and the Book

Joy Wilson was born and bred in Liverpool in the pre-Beatle era. She was at school at Merchant Taylors' and then spent four years at Trinity College, Dublin, reading French and English Literature. A year in France teaching was followed by a few months in Leicester where she met Colin, her writer husband.

She worked as a Librarian in London and then a year after *The Outsider* was published in 1956, they moved to Cornwall - for six months they thought - but they've been here ever since, making their home in Gorran.

Joy made her early debut for Bossiney with a chapter in *Meals for All Seasons,* and then in 1985 contributed to *Westcountry Mysteries.*

Here in *Around St Austell Bay,* she explores, in words accompanied by a wealth of old photographs and picture postcards, an area well-known to her. As she says, '... it has become a familiar, well-loved scene.

'Most of the photographs included here have their own stories to tell of life as it used to be around the Bay. I hope that you will find them as evocative as I do.'

Author Joy Wilson and son Rowan.

Around St Austell Bay

INTRODUCTION

Unless you happen to have been born in one of the places around its shores, or come here by sea, your first view of St Austell Bay is likely to be from the top of an alarmingly steep hill, Penpillick or Hensbarrow, Bodrugan or Polmear.

From any one of these you can see the whole sweep of the bay spread out below, the hilly countryside and dark precipitous cliffs. In the hazy distance the coastline curves gently towards tortoiselike Black Head and the foam-flecked sea is a subtle shade of aquamarine seen nowhere else. White puffs of smoke rise from the chimneys of the clay dries at Par, like distant plumes of cotton wool.

Inland, the land rises up to the rugged moors behind St Austell town, the summits crowned with the rounded shapes of the clay burrows, greened over now with plants, and changed from their former gleaming white cones by a new technology.

It is only eight nautical miles across the choppy waters of the bay between the high rocky shoulder of the Dodman in the south and the sheltered lee of Gribben head to the north. But if you travel on land by the coastal roads around the bay the journey will be almost forty miles.

On the way you will pass the age-old fishing villages, Mevagissey, Gorran Haven, Pentewan and Polkerris; hidden away down quiet tracks are the remoter coves and beaches, Colona, Ropehaven and Vault. Then there is the bustle of the newer ports, Charlestown and Par, built by speculators to serve the mining and clay trades, to profit from the wealth of minerals underground.

The sheltered places around the edge of the bay have always provided refuge. Bronze Age man scratched a living on its shores, the early Celts built their defensive cliff castles on the promontories high above the sea. Trading for tin at Carclaze, mined there since time immemorial, the Phoenicians beached their craft on the nearby sandy shores. On Carn Gray outcrop, facing toward the eastern

Right: *'Mevagissey life has centred around the harbour ...'*

FY228

horizon, they are said to have made sacrifice to the sun god, Baal, for a safe return to their distant home.

Tin, copper, fish and clay have provided a livelihood for the people living here, creating fortunes for a few, and heartbreak for some. It was only just over a hundred years ago that the pilchard finally deserted this bay and the mining bonanza in tin and copper came to an end.

The sailing ships crowded the harbours no more as the new century progressed and new roads and railways brought a growing flood tide of tourists from distant towns. The small fishing villages found themselves getting used to a lot of new faces and an early guide-book recommended to intrepid sight-seers a motor tour round the clay works as a premier excursion.

Right: *Mining tin at Carclaze.*

Left: *Early tourists take a motor tour around the clayworks.*

A more recent visitor, I first came to this part of Cornwall on an overloaded bike with uncertain brakes for a three-day seaside stay. First, a tent in a green meadow above Gorran. Then, by a poet friend, we were offered the lease of his cottage tucked away near the edge of the bay. Through this unlikely chain of events, we have now made our home here for over twenty-five years.

Over all that time, for me, it has become a familiar, well-loved scene. Much has changed: the busier wider roads, villages doubled in size, more people drawn here to live on the fringe of the bay. Reluctantly the old close-knit village communities have faced inevitable change.

But leave the noisy main roads and venture down one of the ancient high-banked lanes, narrow woodland tracks or cliff-edge paths and with a little exploring you can find the essence of this lovely part of Cornwall still unchanged. Hidden sometimes, but never very far away you

DANGEROUS
TO CYCLISTS

On Carn Gray the Phoenicians are said to have worshipped.

can find a deserted enginehouse, a watermill, a smugglers' cellar off a cobbled village street, or an old saint's well.

Assembling this varied collection of photographs and postcards from so many generous local people, sometimes with fascinating reminiscences as well, has been a very exciting experience. Grouped together in the book, I hope that they may capture something of that not so distant past around St Austell Bay.

In one or two of the photographs here you can see that life was not as easy as we would nostalgically like to imagine. There are signs of hard times as well as feast teas and parades.

Left: *'This hill is dangerous to cyclists' is the caption to this 1904 postcard. I, too, first came to this part of Cornwall on a bike.*

A magnifying glass can become a peepshow, bringing the details alive: a lady's hat, a wartime poster, a soldier's uniform. All sorts of different events are here to be found: an election, a funeral, a murder, a derailment, a beauty parade, perhaps all a little different from today.

At a time when a camera was still a rarity and a complication to use, the pioneer photographers created an evocative record of everyday life in the area. There was Herbert Hughes, who in the early 1900s came each summer from his Midland town with camera and tripod to record the local fishing harbours and Cornish seascapes.

Living at St Blazey there was S. Dalby

Ropehaven: 'Hidden away down quiet tracks are the remoter coves and beaches...'

Smith, who ran a little photographic shop there and used what spare time he had in photographing the minutiae of local streets and events.

There was Coath of St Austell and S. T. Govier with his travelling Photovan, who in the 1900s visited all around the bay, both specialising in portraits and street groups and scenes.

Much more recently, we have the faithful record of the wartime years and after, created by the camera of the late George Ellis, a dedicated freelance, who for a time in the early 1940s was the only photo-journalist in Cornwall.

But perhaps the most nostalgic of all are the snaps taken by many an early tourist here on holiday, and postcards found in treasured collections of long ago. Included here you will find a few photographs taken from an old album of 1910, souvenir of a holiday spent at Polpay Farm, Par, and given as a keepsake to the host and his family. The years have passed and, found only by chance a few months ago, this album was retrieved from the debris in a local skip by an inquisitive and appreciative passerby.

Most of the photographs included here have their own stories to tell of life as it used to be around the Bay. I hope that you will find them as evocative as I do.

The Pentewan Railway Annual Sunday School Excursion en route from St Austell, under the overhanging trees of the Pentewan valley, for a day on the grassy towans of the Winnick by the sea. Trucks, especially fitted with benches, were filled with excited children, their parents and teachers, often the only holiday they had. Entertainment included the band, a special picnic tea and the engine-driver's dog eager for games on the sand.

GORRAN HAVEN

Haymaking in the 1930s at Lamledra Farm. In the background is the Dodman, highest land in the area guarding the southern part of St Austell Bay. On its summit long ago, a beacon flared. Lit by local men, it warned of the massed ships of the Spanish Armada, sheltering overnight in its lee for a final council of war.

'Charlie's Paint Mine' – red ochre works with a network of tunnels burrowing into the cliff at Great Perhaver. The landing stage, perched on the rocky outcrop, was used to ship the ochre round to the Haven. Alas, the venture never really paid and little trace remains, but the graceful structure attracted the camera of Dalby Smith.

Gorran Haven from the beach.On the left overlooking the beach are the fish cellars. Alongside is the Watch House, once used by the Coastguards, and next the lime kiln. The little church of St Just looks out to sea, its fifteenth-century tower originally intended to house a guiding light for local ships.

The Haven without a quay. Previous quays, perhaps as many as six, were all in time destroyed by the sea. The first had been built by the Bodrugan family to make a safe harbour for their ships. In 1885, Squire Williams sited a strong new quay on Cadicrowse rocks to benefit local fishermen and shelter the Haven from south-easterly gales. It is still there today.

Dick Pill's Boatyard – 1900s. Gorran-built boats were thought highly of as far away as the east coast. The little bark house for preserving the nets is on the left while the lime kiln, still in use, is also a good vantage point, just as today.

Right: **The Haven children on Fishermen's Beach – hats to protect frcm the sun, bare feet for paddling. Several are in charge of younger brothers or sisters.**

Left: **The quay, 1909 – photographed by Herbert Hughes. Trammel nets were used in spring to catch crabs. Any gavricks or spider crabs caught were free to all and left on the quay for locals to help themselves. Gorran men were expert crabbers and the pots here, made from local withies, were sought after from as far as Devon and Ireland. Questioned in 1889, no Cornish fisherman could explain exactly how the lobsters got into these pots.**

SAB-B

Church Street, 1920s. The Gorran Haven Methodist Annual Parade through the village. The small man walking in front of the band is Tommy Kitto, 'not quite zackly' but a village favourite. Afterwards there was a teafight in a nearby meadow.

The man in Church Street is bringing home his dinner from the communal bakehouse, then situated in Zion Cottage a little way down the hill. Few had ovens of their own.

Canton 1927. Outside the old grist mill, Tommy Kitto stands beside the little river, filled-in in 1935. On the wall he rests his can of drinking water from the pump. Henry Hunkin has parked his motorbike and the road shows more evidence of horses than cars.

In the 1930s.
Left: **Crabbers at the end of the quay.**
Below left: **Gorran Haven Parliament.**
Below: **August on Fishermen's beach – a solitary summer visitor.**

PORT MELLON

Harvesting in the 1930s – on land that once formed part of Sir Henry de Bodrugan's demesne. Bodrugan Barton is built on the site of his old castle and nearby on the cliff is the place where he leapt down on his horse to escape his enemies in a boat to France.

Right: Haymaking in 1892 at Bodrugan Barton. This was one of the last farms in the country to use oxen. Sure footed on steep slopes and always worked in the same pairs, on the farm their names are still remembered: Neat and Comely, Brisk and Lively, Youth and Beauty, Good Luck and Speedwell.

Colona Beach and Chapel Point – a postcard of the twenties. It shows the Point before the houses were built there from stones gathered on the beach. The raised site of the mediaeval chapel can still be seen. From its pointed window the legend tells of Tristan's leap to escape the avenging King Mark. On the beach below stone flints and scrapers have been found, proof of early human habitation on the shores of the bay.

·CHOLERA·AT· MEVAGISSEY,·IN·CORNWALL·
·ENCAMPMENT·OF·THE·INHABITANTS·AT·PORT·MELLON·

·a· MR·KENDALL'S·CELLARS·
·b· OTHER·CELLARS·
·c· HOSPITAL – RECENTLY·AN·INN·
·D· CELLARS·
·E· ENCAMPMENT·OF·ORDNANCE·TENTS·
·F·G·H· COTTAGES·OCCUPIED·BY·REFUGEES·
·i· BAY·OF·MEVAGISSEY·

·from·Illustrated·London·News·25·August·1849·

Right: **Port Mellon in the 1900s – not much change from the 1849 print. There is no road across the beach and the Rising Sun Inn has become a temperance house. The fish cellars were built on land that is now partly under the sea.**

Left: **A print of 1849. In July 1849 cholera was brought to Mevagissey by a returning sailor, Rundle by name. Within a week or two the death toll was so high that the inhabitants took flight over the hill to the healthier air of Port Mellon. Tents were provided but accommodation in the fish cellars across the stream was denied them. Mr Kendall, the owner, believed that the flowing water could prevent the spread of infection into Gorran Parish. Only after a wholesale clean up of Mevagissey's insalubrious streets did the epidemic end and tents were no longer needed.**

Right: **Still no road across the beach and a sandy crossing for an early car.**

Mevagissey's first Lifeboat, *The South Warwickshire,* in 1869. Pictured here just prior to the launching ceremony, her sturdy crew raise the oars in salute. It took place before 3000 enthusiastic people with bands, and flags waving. Later, called out for the first time, the boat had to be relaunched after mountainous seas had thrown her back on shore. The crew of local fishermen then rowed her out in the teeth of the gale, even after some of their oars had been swept away. They fought on to rescue the shipwrecked crew and beached her finally on Par Sands, dizzy themselves with cold and fatigue.

GORRAN CHURCHTOWN

Gorran Churchtown in 1880 – a photograph taken to give to a nostalgic resident exiled up country. The same cottages cluster round the church today but in this view many are still thatched. The road, unpaved, is quiet enough to leave a small cart unattended. Just around the corner is the old stable where the horses of the visiting mailcart from St Austell took their daily rest before the long drive home.

Gorran Church. The crenellated tower was for many years a mark for shipping. The church was rebuilt in the fifteenth century on the site of a much earlier one and stands within the original Celtic Lan, perhaps that of St Goran himself.
The Church House standing at right angles to the church still has its diamond window panes. It housed the Dame School, which provided an education of sorts to those children of the parish able to afford twopence a week. Eventually 137 pupils crowded in. No wonder that the new School Inspectors reported poor progress and the vicar expressed alarm at childish incursions into the graveyard.

'Schoolhouse in the Wind'. In 1880 this new school was built high on the hill overlooking the sea. Conditions were spartan with little shelter from the gales, pumped water and drainage a mere trench behind a hedge. But the new master, Mr Treneer, was a dedicated teacher, and in later years his daughter Ann was to write a well-known book about the school and her childhood days in the parish.

Right: **The Infant Class in 1906, with Mr Brittan, the new headmaster, and Miss Martin again. A strict regime, but the smallest girls are allowed their toys, and young Leo Kendall on the back row sports an imposing watch and chain. Also in the picture are five members of the Whetter family: Howard, Olive, Winifred, Ada and Helen.**

Mr Joe Treneer and his staff in 1897. On his left, the pupil-teacher Alfred Trewin, on the right, standing, is Miss Martin, friend of Ann Treneer. The photo is signed 'S. V. Govier - Photovan', presumably a horse-drawn equipage.

Left: **Miss Ada Maude Richards in 1898, an enterprising young lady, who until she married at age 24, ran the Barley Sheaf at Gorran with her sister quite unaided.**

The Badger Hunt at Gorran was traditionally held on Boxing Day, but here it seems to be summer. Local farmers co-operate, inspecting setts at Tregondean, Sentries and Cruggans Brake. A matter of humane control not indiscriminate Ministry gas. Note the eager terriers and badger tongs. Underneath the photo, named from left to right, are: Stan Whetter, ?, Fred Whetter, Charles Henry Whetter, Fred Michell, 'Capt. Bill' Kendall, Willy Hill, and Lanyon Nicholls. In front: Jacob Kitto, Joseph Nicholls and Nipper the dog.

ST EWE

St Ewe Church – a 1930 postcard sent by a local farmer's wife to her friend in Gorran parish, 'Hope to see you at the cricket on Saturday.'
The spire of the church is crowned with a golden weathervane, set there in 1696. During the past 300 years it has only needed gilding twice. Over the stone sheep grid at the church stile and leaning against the churchyard wall, an ironic gravestone reads:

Time was we's stood where thou do't now
And view the dead as thou dost we
Ere long thoust lay as low as we
And others stand to look on thee.

St Ewe village street, photographed in 1940 by Mr Ellis. It remains much the same today. The Crown Inn was once thatched. Trade was brisk in the nineteenth century when during the tin boom a floating population of 1000 lodged in the area. Many tramped six miles to work at local mines: Happy Union, Wheal Virgin and Great Polgooth.

The ancient cross in the foreground is so old that it is not orientated to the village as it is today. In its time it has served as a support for delinquents in the stocks, a mounting block and a platform for the auctioneer at St Ewe Fair.

Heligan House – pictured in Edwardian times – home of the Tremayne family, Squires of St Ewe and Mevagissey for nearly 400 years. The bricks of which the house is built are a lovely rose red, made from clay dug and fired on the estate. Old account books show that there were two workers who did the job, paid by the foot of house wall built. On completing their task a quart of rum each was the liberal reward.

Inside Heligan house – a view of the stairwell with the family coat of arms and motto, *Honori et Honestas.* **The carved wood escutcheon came from over the porch of the earlier Elizabethan house that stood on this spot. The splendid tapestry behind the pillars was discovered by chance when a wrap was sought to cosset an ailing dog.**

Heligan Mill. Many old tracks through the woods meet at the 400 year old grist mill. When this picture was made the waterwheel still turned with a leisurely creak and the miller on his black mare delivered the sacks of bran. Nowadays he has gone but for Mevagissey folk the little hamlet remains a favourite destination for a walk.

Richard Frederick Michell of St Ewe parish harvesting with a binder at Trelewack Barton. Tinker, Tiger, and Violet over against the corn.

MEVAGISSEY

Ever since the first pier was built in the fifteenth century, Mevagissey life has centred around the harbour, the whitewashed cottages climbing steeply up the hills as though eager for a good view of the activity below. Winding narrow streets and hidden alleys, some still cobbled with stones from the beach, are little changed from Napoleonic times. Then, the prosperity boom in the fishing and smuggling trades caused the harbour to double in size, and local boatyards built some of the fastest luggers in the country, very unpopular with the Preventive Men.

View over the inner harbour and village in the 1900s: the lugger fleet, brown sails furled, moored to floating logs in orderly rows; the topsail schooner dries her sails. On the left-hand quay, three-masters would land the best rough salt from France for fish curing, and coal on the jettyhead. Nets dry over the harbour wall, while along the hill behind Cliff Street is the Ropewalk. There a young lad with the heart of the rope stretched taut round his waist could earn a useful sixpence for an afternoon's work.

Right: **Inner harbour 1909. Preparing for the evening tide, photographed by Herbert Hughes, the pioneer photographer from a midland town, who came each summer to record with a loving eye the seascapes and harbours of Cornwall.**

FY284

Fish Auction on Jetty Head, 1909.

Right: **'Fishing Fleet going out'. A popular postcard of the '20s, it was also issued with the more sombre caption, 'Leaving for another night's toil'. The fishing fleet leaving at sunset from the outer harbour was a sight many would walk out along the quay to see. On a winter's night, the fishing lights of the drifters could be seen sparkling like a necklace strung out along the horizon.**

Upalong, Cliff Street, 1909, a favourite place to watch the weather and activities on the quay. Further up Cliff Street was the chute leading down to the harbour known as 'Bucket and Chuck It', the only solution to village sewage disposal until post World War II.

AND

PILCHARDS IN OIL.

Recommended for Children and Invalids.

ORDER THROUGH YOUR GROCER AND
SUPPORT A HOME INDUSTRY.

Sole Manufacturers :

CORNISH SARDINE COMPANY,

MEVAGISSEY, CORNWALL.

Pilchard Advertisement. Left: **Back in Harbour. Emptying the drift net of a record catch.**

Hail Mevagissey with such wonders fraught,
Where boats, and men and trade and stinks are stirring,
And pilchards come in millions to be caught –
Pilchards a thousand times as good as herring.

Peter Pindar

Here's to the health of the Pope may he live to repent,
And add just six months to the terms of his Lent,
And tell all his vassals from Rome to the Poles
That there's nothing like pilchards for saving their souls.

Mrs Rene Lean, aged 69, with her friend, packing pilchards in wooden hogsheads, as they had first learned to do when they were fourteen. Mevagissey-pressed pilchards went traditionally to Italy where they were appreciated on fast days.

View up Church Street – the only road to Pentewan and St Austell until the 1930s. The steep climb up School Hill, past Lawn House, caused heavy carts to take on an extra horse, and coming down, a heavy drag shoe. Passing the baker's window the gentleman with the watch chain is perhaps on his way to Chapel: 'Today is Sunday and we do put on our bit o' best and our chain.'

In this close-knit community, even in the 1900s when some of these pictures were taken, a single visiting 'stranger' could be excitement enough to rush into the street. Nowadays, each summer, a tidal wave of visitors invades the village, the old fishing lofts are all transformed, but still in late autumn, in winter or on a rough spring day the old harbour life returns.

Feast Tea with a specially baked large, curranty, saffron bun for each child.

Left: Mevagissey Wesleyan Feast Parade 1906. It was always held on the Wednesday of Feast Week in June. First, a march with band and banners to the quay for lively hymn singing, perhaps a relic of earlier sea ceremonies, and then grouped on Town Bridge for the traditional photograph, here taken by Dalby Smith.

Right: **Fore Street in the early 1900s. The staff stand outside the old post and telegraph office in the pillared building on the left. Farther down is the dairy, later a café known as the Beehive (danger of being stung there). Facing down the cobbled street is Alma Robins' shop, milliner and draper.**

Cloke's Horse bus, a daily service, pictured here ready to depart on Town Bridge. Long before, in 1849 its predecessor Craggs' Horse bus was denied access to Truro while on a desperate quest for food for starving Mevagissey residents, during the cholera outbreak in the village.

Hicks' Bakehouse – collecting the turkey. There were five communal bakehouses in the village giving good service when private ovens were few.

A sheaf of pasties baked	$\frac{1}{2}$d
A loaf or a dinner	1d
Christmas dinner	6d

Left: **The village pump in 1927. There were only two sources of water in the village at the time apart from a few private wells. Horses drank from the trough. In the background the car is parked outside the new garage, a foretaste of things to come.**

Mevagissey Tennis Club, founded by Doctor Grier, the local medico, here pictured on the back row. Young ladies in well anchored boaters seem to be in the majority.

POLGOOTH

Polgooth means Goosepool, but it is always associated with the mining of tin. Great Polgooth mine was once the most prosperous in the country, and Polgooth a more important town than St Austell. In the 1800s there were mines on all the hills around: Great Polgooth, Wheal Prosper, Wheal Elizabeth and Wheal Davey, later South Polgooth.

South Polgooth mine in the 1920s. Tin was mined here in Elizabethan times, the records say. At no time was the mine any deeper than 300 feet and by the time this photo was taken it was a surface working only. Today the ruined engine house still stands proudly above Five Turnings, but the ore sheds, stamps and rails shown here are fast disappearing under impenetrable brambles and gorse.

Right: 'The Grand Old Man of Polgooth'. Edward Body May, who lived nearly ninety years in the village, was possessed of a phenomenal memory. Until he died in 1919 he could remember clearly back to the prosperous days of mining in the 1830s. He recalled events like the start of the penny post and the Crimean War. A butcher by trade and a staunch Wesleyan, even in his eighties he would ride over to the Hewas Inn at Sticker for an evening out, trusting to his horse for a safe return.

Strathcona – the old Mines' Count House. Leaning out of the unusual glassed-in balcony the local mine captains would weekly auction setts to waiting miners below. A good sett, or section of a mine to work, meant more earnings for the competing teams of independent tributers. This photograph was taken in more recent days when the house became the private home of coachmaker and wheelwright Edward May, here standing in the porch with Florence, his wife Annie and a friend. The house in the centre of Polgooth is more or less unchanged today.

The beautiful, alien landscape of the clay burrows reflecting the light. Nowadays, technology has found a way to 'green' them over and flatten the cones into a sedate uniformity.

Right: **Time for a break – a small lorryload of dried clay blocks packed with rushes in layers en route for harbour or railway.**

A group of young clay workers 'breaking burden' armed with characteristic Cornish shovels at the head of the tramway.

Experienced clay captains proudly pose for the camera. The bowler was the favoured headgear and retirement came late in life.

Clay captain in the usual bowler and black coat directing the work. No high-powered hoses here. Sleds, shovels, and a natural stream, while keeping dry is an impossibility. Only in the twenties were methods more mechanised.

Bal maidens wearing their best aprons instead of the usual hessian because of the camera. Their job was to clean off any mossy stains leaving the blocks a gleaming white. Some earlier claypit owners were reputed to add dolly blue to the clay to get this more marketable result.

ST AUSTELL

The Town seen from West Bridge – an early nineteenth century print – with 'streets nearly as irregular as cow paths on a furzy common', grouped round the old church on the sunny flank of the hill. The unpaved western turnpike dips down to the 400-year-old packhorse bridge. It was the only road to Truro and the west until the new Truro Road was built. The little river is clear enough for fishing and has water enough to turn two mills. A few yards away on the town side stood the old workhouse with the 'madhouse' attached. There, an occasional chained inmate would scare the passerby with a fierce grimace and a rattle of windowbars.

The Market House. A painting of the 1840s shows it newly built. It is flanked on the right by Dr Drake's Academy, an early school and now the Sun Inn. On the left is Harris's Temperance Hotel, quite forgotten today. The premises were taken over by the old *Queen's Head* inn, then striving to live down its reputation as a smugglers' distribution point. Appropriately, just opposite, running under the churchyard was a grim adit; known as 'Black Hole', it was the town lock-up. The Market House at one time accommodated the Council chamber and the Fire Brigade as well as the regular Friday markets, when live pigs and chickens and cows were on sale. From its balcony both Gladstone and Churchill spoke.

Right: **A very old photograph of 1855 showing the Bull Ring area below the churchyard. Here, long ago, bulls were baited for sport. At the head of the street stands the White Lion, a beer and eating house and also parcel office for the Fairy Mail Coach to Plymouth, with its four-horse team. The Georgian town house to the right was built by Charles Rashleigh, originator of Charlestown harbour. Later, the ancient White Hart coaching inn moved from Fore Street to these more commodious premises. Outside, the street is still unpaved and among the waiting carts two gentlemen pose wearing 'Par Stacks', the local name for the fashionable Stovepipe hats of the time.**

Church Street in the 1890s – a waiting coach outside the White Hart, and Coodes Bank has replaced the old *White Lion.* **Built in exuberant style with fashionable red brick it speaks of the new prosperity brought by the china clay trade. The policeman patrols and the crossing sweeper has plenty to do.**

White Hart Interior – this unique Regency wallpaper, handpainted in delicate colours, was commissioned in Italy by Charles Rashleigh showing an unexpected aesthetic streak. The panoramic view of Vesuvius and the Bay of Naples was perhaps intended to compare with the quieter beauties of St Austell Bay.

Clay waggon in Fore Street. For over 100 years the waggons with their teams of three horses negotiated the narrow streets travelling between the clay works in the Higher Quarter and the harbours and railway below. Waggons, struggling to pass each other on the slippery roadway, led to constant hazards for the town's pedestrians. One lady lost her skirt and petticoat – dragged off by a lumbering wheel passing too close.

Clay Strike 1913. Claymen on strike march with their wives in protest down Truro Road. Wages were hardly adequate to raise a family and feelings ran higher than this orderly gathering would suggest. Tough police from Glamorgan (below) **were brought in to pressure the men back to work; equipped with bikes they patrolled the clay district. Financial straits eventually broke the strike and the men went back to work for the same wages. Fortunately, Medland Stocker, a more enlightened employer, arranged a better deal for the men a few months later.**

The Prince and Princess of Wales, later King George V and Queen Mary, made a visit to St Austell including a trip to a clay works. Such was their popularity that a triumphal arch was erected in their honour.

Right: **West End, Fore Street – still unpaved and showing tracks of clay waggons. A line-up of local citizens pose for the camera. The old town smithy is on the right and also the very first post office in the town. It supplanted a lady carrier who distributed the mail on foot with a basket.**

Tidy's Corner and the General Wolfe. Beneath the odd little building housing the tobacconist, W. H. Smith opened their first tiny shop in the town. The sign outside is not their usual one and reads simply *'W. H. Smith – Subscription Library'.* **After only a few months here, in 1906 they moved to much needed larger premises. Next door is the** *Globe Inn* **also housing Warne's the Printers. At the General Wolfe, a real man's pub, the landlady served beer to passing waggon drivers through the window overlooking the road.**

Butcher and Post Office – Tregonissey Lane End, 1900s – a family group photographed by Coath of St Austell. The Kelly family, with many descendants still living in the town, ran the business. Everyone helped: the youngest daughter tackled the cooking perched up on a stool, and another ran a stall in the market. In cold weather on the butcher's van the children were made to run behind to keep warm.

William Box, 1925 – a long established Grocer in Church Street (see reflection in the window). The staff lined up in the dinner hour include: (left to right) William Lemin, Bill Dingle, Maud Chesterfield, Fred Pooley, Ern Rowe, Reg Michael and the errand boy Frank Golley. Mr Box himself had gone off to his lunch.

St Austell people.
John Trudgian, the organ builder setting off on his tricycle in 1889.

J. F. Frost's Music Shop – gramophone horns in the window.

Right: **'The Spider Bridge' – St Austell Railway viaduct and a distant view of the south side of the town. The graceful wooden supports are carrying the Cornwall Railway, known as the railway on stilts. Nowadays there is a more prosaic structure.**

Left: **Clay waggons waiting to unload at the Pentewan Railway terminus at the foot of Foundry Hill.**

PENTEWAN

Pentewan Harbour in the early days of the century. The lady sitting in the sun with her basking dog ignores the bustle below. Crowded with ships the little harbour has not yet lost the final battle with silt. The raised trestle viaduct on the left carries the rails of the little train from St Austell bringing clay to be dropped down through chutes to the waiting holds below. Coal is carried on the train's return journey and before another load of clay the trucks will have to be scrubbed out, an arduous task.

The postcard with the urgent message shows the Dock at work. On the hill is the Regency terrace and church rebuilt by Sir Christopher Hawkins when he created the harbour in 1819. Below, on the quay, the big door leads into the stable once used by the railway horses, and near the lock gates is the harbour-master's house. The small rowing boats are hobblers, used to carry a line to sailing ships waiting to enter harbour. They can then winch themselves in through the tricky harbour entrance. Patient horses wait to load coal on the iron-ore quay.

Right: **A lone fisherman in the mist of early morning prepares his nets.** Below: **A good catch: clearing the seine net on Pentewan beach in the 1950s.**

Floral Dance in the Square in the 1930s.

Left: **Annual Bible Christian outing in the mowhay at Sconhoe Farm. On the right is Theophilous Couch, redoubtable local Shipping Agent, who rode on horseback in all weathers up to the clayworks to secure contracts for his ships. Young Amy Sarah has climbed to the very highest point, while her kid brother Ivor sits cross-legged in front.**

Picnic on Pentewan Breakwater.

Right: A postcard of Black Head showing the double entrenchments of the Iron Age castle defences, and a secluded smuggler's beach below.

Wartime bomb damage in the Square, photographed by George Ellis. Major roof repairs are needed for Prettyman's General Store. In earlier times the family had skippered several local sailing ships. Today windows are shattered all around the Square.

A rare postcard of Trenarren showing the village among the trees. Once it was busy with two pubs and several shops, but nowadays only a scatter of cottages remain. A peaceful retreat for the Cornish poet and historian A. L. Rowse, born in St Austell, whose home now is the old family house of the Hexts, looking down the wooded valley to the sea.

PORTHPEAN

Right: **Porthpean beach in high summer at Regatta time was always a popular outing for St Austell people. The extensive fish cellars have long gone but the big houses with gardens overlooking the sea remain. The house on the extreme right before rebuilding was the old Dolphin Inn.**

Left: **Across the beach is the yellow overgrown cliff where, in 1952, two murders were committed. Obsessed with the idea of visiting a new London girlfriend, Miles Gifford the 26-year-old son of a local solicitor, lost patience with the latter's prohibition on using the family car. When his parents returned to their Porthpean home he attacked both brutally with a heavy pipe and wheelbarrowed their unconscious bodies over the edge of the cliff. Next day they were found dead on the rocks below. Gifford was speedily caught at his insouciant girlfriend's house, after taking the car, when she told the police that she had taken his account of the deed as a fantasy. At the ensuing trial, the sceptical Cornish jury took a different view, rejecting very strong psychiatric evidence of a disturbed personality, and Gifford was condemned to death.**

Miss Gabrielle Vallance, Miles' nineteen-year-old girlfriend, demure in New Look coat on her way to the Court in Bodmin. A photo by George Ellis.

Women crowding around the car conveying Gifford to Bodmin Assizes.

BISCOVEY, SPIT BEACH, TREGREHAN, CRINNIS

Lodge Hill Cottages, Biscovey. Although they seem to have been sturdily built they have been pulled down. Once they stood beside the school. The lady standing in the first doorway was named Jenkins and later committed suicide by throwing herself down a mine shaft on the golf links. Her body was eventually found on Spit Beach below.

Right: **Tregrehan House, 200-year-old home of the Carlyon family. A wartime auction is taking place to raise funds for the Red Cross. Above the colonnade the children of the family survey the treasures displayed below.**

Spit Cafe, Par, on the way to Spit Beach, was a favourite place for a family outing. Behind the rails is a place for prams and bikes. Note the predecessor of the pushchair with its charming occupant. A hot day but one lady has brought her furs!

Crinnis, Carlyon Bay – judging a Bathing Beauty contest just after the second World War. Bikinis are a daring innovation and the result of the contest is perhaps not to *everyone's* **satisfaction.**

CHARLESTOWN

In 1791, the first sheltering harbour wall was constructed on the sands of West Polmear. Behind it the inner harbour basin was excavated out of the solid rock of the cliff by local men with only picks and shovels and mules to clear the debris. In less than two years the little port was ready for ships, one of the first floating harbours in the country, controlled by lock gates and a special leat for water levels. It was named after the local squire and speculator, Charles Rashleigh, who had the enterprise to plan a safe sea outlet to markets far away for the ore from twenty local mines and the evolving china clay trade nearby. Round about the harbour the picturesque terraces of the new village were built, little altered today.

Here in the 1900s the masts of sailing ships crowd the basin, making the harbour look much as it did in Charles Rashleigh's day. Today a schooner is a rarity except when a film is being made, but the little port is busier than ever.

From the clayworks in the Higher Quarter behind St Austell town, down through the tortuous narrow streets and on to Charlestown Harbour came the heavily laden two-ton waggons piled with china clay. So familiar was the route and reliable the teams of horses, that if he wished a driver could leave his waggon for a quick beer en route. With the help of a short cut or two across hedges he could easily catch up with the team again still plodding the churned up road.

Below: The old order changeth. . . first of the mechanised vehicles that gradually took over from the horses. Much less mess but bigger loads and solid wheels still took heavy toll of the roads.

Right: **Mount Charles 1900s. No clay waggons on the road today and a good turnout for the Bethel Bible Christian Sunday School parade. Big bunches of bananas, a newly imported novelty, hang on the standings to tempt young appetites.**

Left: **The harbour in 1914, with clay chutes and a covered tramway on the left. Carried straight from the Dry, the clay blocks were shot from specially tilting trucks into the waiting holds below. These chutes are still used today but the tramway and the picturesque mixture of sail and steam are gone.**

TYWARDREATH

Tywardreath means in Cornish the house on the sandy strand, reminiscent of when the tide came close to here.

Right: **Church Street, 1913 – a sunny day for an outing in the trap. Miss Gerrans, the local dressmaker, stands in her doorway for the benefit of the photographer, together with two young friends.**

Left: **Belmont Street, 1913 – F. Johns has climbed into the baker's handcart, while two demure young ladies, May Bartlett and Irene Cole, decide to hurry by.**

ST BLAZEY

Fifteenth century St Blazey Church – a postcard of the 1900s. St Blaise was the patron saint of woolcombers, and of sore throats too. Only 200 years ago the sea swirled close to this churchyard wall. Later, when it receded, the town expanded on the reclaimed sea sand. St Blazey was always a busy place and during the heyday of local mines and granite quarries it became a boom town. With their decline things got harder, but ever since medieval times St Blazey folk have had a reputation for being tough minded.

Floods in Station Road, 1928. All stand clear as the car struggles through. Keeping his camera dry Dalby Smith photographs the alarming surge of water outside his little photographic shop. In the garden stands Mrs Dalby Smith with Miss Wade. Returning from school the children risk wet feet.

Right: **Election, 1906, Station Road. Liberal supporters show their green and red flags. No votes for women yet so only men are involved in this bid to rouse the electors. On the wall of the warehouse an agency sign advertises emigration to the mines of South Africa. A solution to hard times sought by many at that period.**

Left: **West & Sons, St Blazey Foundry – 1889. William West began as a bal boy when his first engineering experience was gained holding a candle as Richard Trevithick worked on the 'Catch me who can' steam locomotive. Later, West helped him to develop the improved Cornish beam engine and opened this foundry. Here he built an improved man-engine with iron rods cast on the spot and designed a very economical 80-inch cylinder engine, both for Fowey Consols mine. A respected man, he stands, here, at an angle to his workforce, some of whom proudly hold the tools of their trade and seem as old as himself. Before state pensions retirement came late.**

Funeral of a Crimean War Veteran – very well attended with a Volunteers band and a party of girls from the Laundry works nearby.

Left: **Recruiting March 1915 – 'Kitchener needs you'. The troops line up in front of the Packhorse Hotel. The band plays inspiring music to attract recruits since enlistment was entirely voluntary so early in the War.**

Annual Works Outing. A happier occasion for the girls from the Laundry. One little boy wears a kilt, and the charabancs, still with acetylene lamps and solid wheels, offer little protection from a shower.

Bridge Street. Mr Kittow's butcher shop is on the corner just as today. The first Co-op in the town opened in the little shop on the right. Down the street on the left the three-storey house with the little child outside was MacNally's Lodging House, known locally as 'Fleapit'.

Co-op store in 1909 in Bridge Street.

Putting in the gas main at Star Corner in 1923. No bulldozers, so this is a labour intensive undertaking, but there is time to stop for the camera. The vicar seems a little anxious at the upheaval outside his churchyard wall.

A. Crago Polkerris AJS 1927	S. Truscott AJS 1927	? Camps AJS 1926	? Camps Royal Enfield 1927	Kitt AJS 1927	L. Camps 1926 Douglas	K. Smith	P. Rose at the pump

Motorcycle Lineup. Photographed by Dalby Smith for a twenties postcard, the boys pose with their machines – all British made. Nearest to the petrol pump on the right is the photographer's son.

Fun at St Blazey. Many comic postcards were produced at St Blazey. Although the sea was two miles away it was still a holiday resort.

A Visit from the Travelling Fair.

PAR

On the wide empty sands of Par, or Porth as it was known, the mines Adventurer, J. T. Treffry, created this artificial tidal harbour for his local enterprises in tin, copper, granite and clay. The top engineers of the day, consulted by him, warned that on an open beach the idea was impractical.
Being a determined man, he paced out his plan of the harbour himself on the wet sand, took borings of the rock of treacherous Spit Reef and there ordered to be constructed a massive curving breakwater of local stone. Studying the shifting sea currents carefully, he planned a safe entrance channel to give mooring to over fifty ships.

It was a success from the start; on the reclaimed marshes alongside the port there were quickly established blacksmiths, ship repairers, lime kilns, coal wharves, timber pickling pits, smelting works and later a flour mill. Par harbour became the local hive of activity, and the village quickly grew where once a ferry crossed the marshy estuary.

Left: **Par Harbour 1890, as its creator might have known it.**

Below: **View over the harbour from Mount in the 1900s. The old farmhouse of Porth is here still thatched. On the hill behind it at Mount stood old Par Consols mine. The chimney of Par Stack and the smelters are on the left, no longer used. Timber and coal for the mines are loaded into the waggons of the tramway and schooners crowd at the quayside.**

Left: **The barquentine *Waterwitch* in full sail – she was the last square-rigger working, her skipper Captain Charles Deacon of Par. On Sundays at sea he would find time to read his Bible whatever the conditions.**

Par Harbour. These small ships carried cargoes to and from distant places, weathering many a storm. Skippers and crews were a tough breed of local men whose knowledge of wind and sea, especially in coastal waters, was unrivalled.

The Committee Boat, Par Regatta, 1910 – all local men in the shipping business, a close-knit group. Wearing a nautical cap on the left is Inkerman Tregaskes, born in 1854, harbourmaster for many years. The stout gentleman in the bowler with Martini action service rifle is Samuel Tregaskes, shareholder in more than a dozen vessels. Leaning on the rope is Captain Sam Tregaskes, skipper of the only harbour steam tug *Treffry*. Left to right: **Mr Stephens of Fowey, Mr Morcom, Inkerman Tregaskes, Mr Rosevear, Mr Pearce, Samuel Tregaskes, R. B. Tregaskes, Noel Purcell and Captain Sam Tregaskes.**

Above right: **Par Stack ready to fall in 1907 – this massive chimney was the vent for the dangerous fumes from the lead smelting works on the harbour. The thousands of bricks of which it was built were made from the sand of the beach. It stood 220 feet tall and once a Fowey sailor called Ambrose won a wager by standing on his head at the very top. The demolition** (right) **made an exciting day out for local people and a spectacular fall it must have been.**

THE LAST OF PAR STACK AUG 23 1907

Right: **Par's first post office in the 1890s, in a house still there opposite the newly-opened station. When the mail was ready one of the young ladies would run across to put it on the train.** From left to right: **P. Lias, Postmaster, Mr Laver, Jim Stephens, Postmen. Blanche Blewett, Mr Dingle, Mr Richards, Mr Stephens, Alf Stephens, Mr Pengelly,** and in front, **Mr Barnecutt, Blamy, Sandy and Miss G. Hewett.**

Left: **Harbour Road, 1908. Mrs Pound the postmistress stands in the doorway of her shop. Oil lamps still light the street and the** *Mercury* **poster brings alarming news of German fleet manoeuvres.**

Par Station Derailment – pausing to consider the damage.

Par Bridge, Harbour Road and Butcher's shop. Mr Northcote, in striped apron stands by his well-filled window. Over the bridge, the low building on the left is his killing house. Upstairs in the window can be seen the steam kettle of his dressmaker lodger.

Left: **Floods at Par Station, early in the 1900s. The low-lying ground made water a frequent hazard. Ganger Bolt surveys his reflection on the down side of the track.**

Tregaskes General Provisions Store, Harbour Road, pre 1908. Mrs Tom Stephens with her infant in the elegant perambulator parked on the roadway.

Right: **SS *Archmor* blown ashore on Par Beach, 25 February 1935.**

Par Carnival Float, 1932. Mr Collings and son Noel and friends get ready for the parade.

A HOLIDAY ALBUM

Records of a pleasant fortnight
spent with Mr & Mrs Martin
at Polsay. July 1910

With best wishes from the party.
Geo. F. Goose Alice M. Goose
Ernest G. Goose Nelly Davy

Loading sand.

On Par Sands.

Picnic at Menabilly.

Picnic in the valley.

POLRIDMOUTH AND GRIBBEN HEAD

View of Gribben Head from Polridmouth. On this beach many smugglers' night-time runs occurred. In places the rocks are worn down by cartwheel tracks. Occasionally, before the days of expert navigation, The Gribben was disastrously mistaken for St Anthony's Head at the entrance to Falmouth Bay. Hence the 100-year-old Daymark on the hill.

Menabilly – the family house of the Rashleighs since Jacobean times. During the 1920s it became for some time the home of the writer, Daphne du Maurier. Her love of the place inspired her to use it as the setting of her novel *Rebecca,* **in which it is renamed** *Manderley.* **The sober eighteenth-century frontage of reality pictured here, belies the extravagance of the romantic edifices used in films of this famous story.**

Left: **In the 1930s on the same beach the sailing vessel,** *Romanie* **came to grief here. Sailing round from Fowey to Par in a thick fog, she failed to clear the treacherous point and struck on the rocks at the end of the beach. The captain stepped safely on to the sand with birdcage in hand, but rough seas soon broke up his ship. Today only fragments of rusty plating remain.**

POLKERRIS

Polkerris harbour photographed by an early tourist in 1910.

Old Coastguard Cottages, Polkerris – a postcard issued by George Ellis in the early forties. Originally these cottages were built by the unpopular Preventive service to house the Riding officers. Their job was to patrol the cliffs on horseback to discourage smuggling. They had to be housed together for their own protection, as in other Cornish seaside places. Later used by the Coastguard Service, the cottages seem to have hardly changed today.

Lifeboat Launching 1908. In 1859, Polkerris was chosen as the earliest lifeboat station on St Austell Bay. Now there is a new lifeboat and a day of celebration. At the end of its working life, this boat was converted into a yacht and still sails today. The massive building behind the line of bunting is the Elizabethan 'fish palace' built to process the huge pilchard catches of former times. The fish have now moved to different waters and these buildings are long gone.

Right: **Sunset at Polkerris – 1912. The schooner** *Voltaire* **aground, with an ebbing tide.**

The SV *Voltaire,* **after running aground in the harbour, 1912. A French ship on her way to Par Harbour, she is here being rescued by the steam tug,** *Countess of Jersey.* **In the village there have been some changes. On the site of the old fish cellars, the lifeboat house has been built. The big square door with spectators in front, hides the coastguards' gig, and the building is nowadays the Rashleigh Arms. But here the old village pub was called the General Elliott, after the defender of Gibraltar, and is the long building on the left facing squarely across the bay, with an interested crowd of customers peering over the harbour wall.**

Also Available

WESTCOUNTRY MYSTERIES
Introduced by Colin Wilson
A team of authors probe mysterious happenings in Somerset, Devon and Cornwall.
Drawings and photographs all add to the mysterious content.
'A team of authors have joined forces to re-examine and probe various yarns from the puzzling to the tragic.'
James Belsey, Bristol Evening Post

THE MOORS OF CORNWALL
by Michael Williams
Contains 77 photographs and drawings. The first ever publication to incorporate the three main moorland areas of Cornwall.
'... is not only a celebration in words of the Moors and their ancient pagan stones and granite strewn tors but a remarkable collection of photographs and drawings of Penwith, Goss and Bodmin Moors ...'
Sarah Foot, The Editor, Cornish Scene.

WEST CORNWALL IN THE OLD DAYS
by Douglas Williams. 150 photographs.
St Ives, Mousehole, Newlyn, Penzance, St Just, Helston and Mullion are only some of the places featured in this nostalgic book. Richly illustrated.
'This book has something of a celebratory feel about it. Mr Williams, a Bard of the Cornish Gorsedd, has produced a thoroughly delightful volume, packed with a splendid selection of photographs that span the mid-nineteenth century to the present day ...'
Dr James Whetter, The Cornish Banner

COASTLINE OF CORNWALL
by Ken Duxbury
Ken Duxbury has spent thirty years sailing the seas of Cornwall, walking its clifftops, exploring its caves and beaches, using its harbours and creeks. Over 100 photographs, 45 in colour.
'... a trip in words and pictures from Hawker's Morwenstow in the north, round Land's End and the Lizard to the gentle slopes of Mount Edgcumbe country park.'
The Western Morning News

FOWEY – RIVER AND TOWN
by Sarah Foot
An enlarged and updated edition of Following the River Fowey.
'The intricate tapestries of this delightful area is woven together with warm, understanding interviews... buy, beg or borrow it.'
The Cornish Times

UNKNOWN CORNWALL
by Michael Williams
84 drawings and photographs nearly all especially commissioned for this publication, portraying features of Cornwall rarely seen on the published page.
'... a treasure chest of rich jewels that will surprise many people who pride themselves on a thorough knowledge ...'
Western Evening Herald

100 YEARS ON BODMIN MOOR
by E. V. Thompson. 145 photographs.
A rich harvest of old photographs and picture postcards, reflecting life on the Moor for a century with perceptive text.
'... will entice the present day visitor to Cornwall to explore the Moor ...'
Pamela Luke, The Methodist Recorder

PEOPLE AND PLACES IN CORNWALL
by Michael Williams
Featuring Sir John Betjeman, Marika Hanbury Tenison, Barbara Hepworth and seven other characters, all of whom contributed richly to the Cornish scene.
'... outlines ten notable characters... whose lives and work have been influenced by ''Cornwall's genius to fire creativity''... a fascinating study.'
The Cornish Guardian

HEALING, HARMONY & HEALTH
by Barney Camfield
Healing in its various forms, the significance of handwriting and dreams, and psycho-expansion.
'If you are tuned in to the right wave length of new age thinking... you won't want to put it down until you get to the last page.'
David Rose, Western Evening Herald

MYSTERIES IN THE DEVON LANDSCAPE
by Hilary Wreford & Michael Williams
Outstanding photographs and illuminating text about eerie aspects of Devon. Seen on TSW and Channel 4. Author interviews on DevonAir and BBC Radio Devon.
'... a fascinating book. But it is worth getting just for the superb pictures ...'
Express & Echo

PEOPLE & PLACES IN DEVON
by Monica Wyatt
Dame Agatha Christie, Sir Francis Chichester, Dr David Owen, Prince Charles and others. Monica Wyatt writes about eleven famous people who have contributed richly to the Devon scene.
'A very interesting title from this rapidly expanding publishing house. Indeed, for a ''cottage'' industry it's going from strength to strength, its territory now covering an area from Bristol to Land's End.'
Irene Roberts, The South Hams Newspapers

SOMERSET IN THE OLD DAYS
by David Young. 145 old photographs.
David Young of TSW takes a journey in words and old pictures across Somerset.
'Scores of old photographs of good quality and high human interest... Excellent value... It is narrated by David Young, Television South West's architectural pundit, and his captions are usually eye-catching and informative.'
Drew Brodbeck,
Gloucestershire and Avon Life

STRANGE SOMERSET STORIES
Introduced by David Foot with chapters by Ray Waddon, Jack Hurley, Lornie Leete-Hodge, Hilary Wreford, David Foot, Rosemary Clinch and Michael Williams.
'Publisher Michael Williams has tried to capture an essence of the Westcountry bizzare ...'
Peter John,
Bath and West Evening Chronicle

LEGENDS OF SOMERSET
by Sally Jones. 65 photographs and drawings.
Sally Jones travels across rich legendary landscapes. Words, drawings and photographs all combine to evoke a spirit of adventure.
'... an entertaining look at county tales that have long inspired chill or chuckle.'
Somerset County Gazette

UNKNOWN SOMERSET
by Rosemary Clinch and Michael Williams
A journey across Somerset, visiting off-the-beaten-track places of interest. Many specially commissioned photographs by Julia Davey add to the spirit of adventure.
'Somerset has been called the ''County of Romantic Splendour'', and the two authors have explored many of the less well-known aspects of the countryside and written about them with enthusiasm.'
Somerset and Avon Life

LEGENDS OF CORNWALL
by Sally Jones. 60 photographs and drawings.
Brilliantly illustrated with photographs and vivid drawings of legendary characters. A journey through the legendary sites of Cornwall, beginning at the Tamar and ending at Land's End.
'Highly readable and beautifully romantic...'
Desmond Lyons, Cornwall Courier

KING ARTHUR COUNTRY in CORNWALL
THE SEARCH for the REAL ARTHUR
by Brenda Duxbury, Michael Williams and Colin Wilson.
Over 50 photographs and 3 maps.
An exciting exploration of the Arthurian sites in Cornwall and Scilly, including the related legends of Tristan and Iseult, with The Search for the Real Arthur by Colin Wilson.
'... provides a refreshing slant on an old story linking it with the present.'
Caroline Righton. The Packet Newspapers

AROUND LAND'S END
Michael Williams explores the end and the beginning of Cornwall. Wrecks and legends, the Minack Theatre, Cable & Wireless, Penwith characters and customs, lighthouses and Lyonesse all feature. 90 photographs, many of them from Edwardian and Victorian times, help to tell the story.
'... a delightful stroll not only along the lanes but the legends of this celebrated area.'
The Cornishman

MOUNT'S BAY
by Douglas Williams
More than 120 old photographs of an area stretching from Land's End to the Lizard with perceptive text by one of Cornwall's most respected journalists.
'... a fascinating and exhaustive study... It is a guidebook, potted history, pictorial gallery of Cornish life – all these things and very much more.'
The Western Evening Herald

THE CORNISH COUNTRYSIDE
by Sarah Foot. 130 illustrations, 40 in colour.
Here, in Bossiney's first colour publication, Sarah Foot explores inland Cornwall, the moors and the valleys, and meets those who work on the land.
'Sarah Foot sets out to share her obvious passion for Cornwall and to describe its enigmas... It is a book for those who are already in love with Cornwall and for those who would like to know her better.'
Alison Foster, The Cornish Times

RIVERS OF CORNWALL
by Sarah Foot. 130 photographs, 45 in colour.
The author explores six great Cornish rivers: the Helford, the Fal, the Fowey, the Camel, the Lynher and the Tamar.
'... makes use of many colour illustrations as well as black and white and shows that whatever changes may have taken place in the river economics they remain places of quality and beauty, quintessentially Cornwall.'
The Cornish Guardian

NORTH CORNWALL IN THE OLD DAYS
by Joan Rendell, 147 old photographs.
These pictures and Joan Rendell's perceptive text combine to give us many facets of a nostalgic way of North Cornish life, stretching from Newquay to the Cornwall/Devon border.
'This remarkable collection of pictures is a testimony to a people, a brave and uncomplaining race.'
Pamela Leeds, The Western Evening Herald

SEA STORIES OF CORNWALL
by Ken Duxbury, 48 photographs.
'This is a tapestry of true tales', writes the author, 'by no means all of them disasters – which portray something of the spirit, the humour, the tragedy, and the enchantment, that is the lot of we who know the sea.'
'Ken is a sailor, and these stories are written with a close understanding and feel for the incidents.'
James Mildren, The Western Morning News

A CORNISH CAMERA
by George Ellis and Sarah Foot.
More than 200 photographs taken by George Ellis, the doyen of Cornish press photographers: Cornwall at work and play in war and peace; town and countryside and coast; personalities and customs; triumphs and tragedies. Sarah Foot's text adds the stories behind these pictures.
'A delightful nostalgic look back at the last 40 years in the County.'
Sunday Independent